Malik al Mawt

Richard Tabler

Manufactured in the United States of America. Copyright 2024 by Cadmus Publishing LLC. All rights reserved. No part of this book may be reproduced in any form, audio, digital, or in print, except excerpts by reviewers, without written permission from the copyright holder or Cadmus Publishing LLC.

Published by Cadmus Publishing LLC.
P. O. Box 8664. Haledon, NJ 07538
Web: Cadmuspublishing.com
Web: BooksByPrisoners.com
Business email: admin@cadmuspublishing.com
Author email: info@cadmuspublishing.com
Phone: 360.565.6459

ISBN# 978-1-63751-447-4
Book Catalog Info Categories: True Crime/Autobiography
Library of Congress Control Number: 2024939386

CadmusPublishing.com

Richard Tabler

TABLE OF CONTENTS

Prelude..vii

Chapter 1 Retaliation...1

Chapter 2 You're Not Forgotten...13

Chapter 3 Cover Up...43

Chapter 4 Recognizing Real & Honest Officers...............49

Chapter 5 The End...53

RICHARD TABLER

"We all have pasts
We all made choices that
Maybe weren't the best
Ones. None of us are
Completely innocent
But we get a fresh start
Everyday to be a
Better person
Than we were
yesterday."

RICHARD TABLER

PRELUDE

On the evening of March 21st- 2023, I got a surprise that was long overdue and completely unexpected. I had been housed since January 2nd-2011. Please take note that if you are an emotional person or very religious and cannot keep an open mind while you are reading. You might want to pass this book on to someone else, because, from this point forward, my words may very well become offensive. This is because, I have never honestly learned how to let go of the pain, suffering, and rage that I feel towards those who not only were responsible for my well-being inside of prison but allowed others to dictate their actions and abuse their standings in life. The cruel and unusual punishment goes further than you could under- stand.

It's here that I have decided to share just what I went through and who was behind it all and why. My name is Richard L. Tabler, but my friends and enemy alike also know me by my nickname, "Blue". What you hold in your hands is the writing of the uncut and raw ver- sion of my life from an inside account of my first time being in pris- on in the state of Texas. How things are done here is different from how they are done and run in California and Florida. Texas gives a new defin - tion to the words "Cruel and Unusual Punishment".

My real trouble didn't start until October of 2008. Sure, most would think that it started the day I went to prison with a sentence of death, but though that might be true in someone's eyes, it's not the case here. I knew I was destined to spend my life in prison from a very young age. That telling is for another time and place, which this being, is not that time.

All names of people within the following are real names and used as they should be, for we all are responsible for our actions. Going back and speaking about the unspoken is never an easy thing to do when it caused someone so much pain and heartache, so I ask that you please bear with me as I walk you through the injustice that is done by the Texas Department of Criminal Justice and even at the hands of the Attorney General, District Attorney's and a lone and sorry piece of shit, who so happened to be at the time a State Senator and a part of the Texas Department of Criminal Justice Board. These are my words and mine alone…This is the story of "Malik-al-Mawt".

CHAPTER 1
"Retaliation"

On September 30th- 2018, I was driven back to Bell, County Texas, and the District court for a hearing. During this hearing, I was waiving my rights to further appeals and volunteering for execution. Upon my re- turn to death row, which is located at the Polunsky Unit in Livingston, Texas. I was returned to F-Pod. This all took place on the same day.

During the week of October, I was in E-Dayroom on F-Pod when in came an escort team with a Sergeant, and between the three (3) of these Correctional Officers was an Ad-Seg inmate in leg irons and handcuffs behind his back. Not thinking anything of it, I continued to mind my own business, but that all changed the minute I heard what sounded like someone beating a piece of meat in a butcher shop. Try- ing to find where the sound was coming from and the moans of pain. I looked over towards the D-section which I could do from the E-Dayroom, and took notice of the door open at #43 cage which is right next to the shower and cross-over door.

What I saw seared into my brain to this very day. I saw the Ad-Seg inmate that had passed by me just moments before with a sergeant and two escorting offi ers beating the shit out of in this cage now, with the riot batons carried by the escorting team and what's worse was it was the sergeant wailing off on this dude. Don't forget this prisoner is in restraints and is unable to protect himself in any way or fashion. After the Sergeant and his two correctional officers were done beating this man, they walked out of the cell, leaving this prisoner beaten and in shackles and handcuffs without medical attention.

Unable to sleep that night, I listened to see if anyone would go to the down Ad-Seg prisoner. I started thinking about what I could do to make sure something like this didn't happen to me or someone I knew. Not seriously thinking things through, I borrowed another inmate's cell phone and made some calls.

Before I knew it, I was on the phone with someone I met when I was in the free world and at a party at the 4th ID Barracks on Fort Hood Military Base in Killeen, Texas. From there, I was calling directly to another person's cell phone from my Texas Death Row cell to none other than State Senator John Whitmire (unknown to me at the time, was that this man was also part of the TDCJ-ID Board). Talking to this asshole about treatment and confinemen . It wasn't long before things were twisted around, and I was now this convicted killer asking him for help with my appeals and visiting with my family.

Not only was nothing he said true, but this piece of shit would go to extremes to abuse his place of authority just to use me and mine as an example. John Whitmire is a criminal just like everyone in prison, but he's even worse and still has to this day, fooled so many people. He used the Office of Inspector General for his own gain and lied about many things.

One thing I want you to stop and think about please is this... back in 2008, when you had a cell phone, could you take another cell phone and call information requesting an- other cell phone number? Now ask yourself this, how was it possible for me to be talking to "then" State Senator, John Whitmire directly from the cell phone I was using to his own personal cell phone? Just as the current criminal who is finding himself in court now, Attorney General Ken Paxton, well though I'm getting ahead of myself in this book, John Whitmire should be investigated because trust me, he's dirty and in some of the worst possible ways. So, after calling this shit bag and things being turned against myself and my loved ones, I was placed into total isolation by the Director and the orders of John Whit- mire.

Each Pod in the 12-building where Texas Death Row prisoners are housed has a total of 84 single-man cells (cages). These cells are cut into sections of 14-single man cells, starting from A-F with a day- room in front of our cages, in handcuffs behind our backs, and under escort by two correctional officer . Each cage has a stainless-steel toilet and sink combo, a metal desk with a shelf above it, and a metal bunk with a 1 ¼ thick plastic mattress that's no longer than 6 feet long. I was taken from

F-pod and moved to A-Pod, B-section #26 cage around the end of October/2008.

Once I was escorted by tons of rank to this cage and section, I was instructed after the leg irons were removed to slowly get up and place my handcuffed hands through the food slot to be removed. Once this was done, I was further instructed to give up my boxers, which I did as well. Thus, im now butt-ass naked in a cage with NOTHING. I was given a mattress, no sheets, no blanket, no toilet tissue, and no clothing. Let me remind you that it's also currently wintertime and the temp outside is freezing. The air conditioner is blowing full blast into my cage.

Looking around at my living arrangements, I take notice of the video camera mounted above the toilet into the stainless steel, which is watching me twenty-four-seven now as I stand there shivering because I am butt-ass naked. Walking to the door because it's warmer, I take notice that an office has been assigned to sit in front of my cage as well 24/7. The officer has a can of chemical agents, a gas mask, a flashlight, a walkie-talkie (radio), and a cooler for his/her food. Oh, and they are fully dressed and sitting in a chair.

What seemed like a few minutes after I was placed into this cage with no clothing and nothing else… Rank was returning… A lieutenant and a sergeant. They opened my food slot and ordered me to strip out even though I had nothing to give them (butt ass naked). It was all for show, I was then ordered to place my hands out the slot so that I could be placed into handcuffs behind my back.

Once this was done, the cage door was rolled open, and I was instructed to back out. This done, the sergeant entered into the cage and the lieutenant and officer watching me stood with me on the rim butt naked as the sergeant went through my cage. Once this was done, I was allowed to enter back into the cage and the cuffs were removed. The light was turned on from the control picket, thus I was unable to turn the light off at any time.

For the next month and change, every 15 minutes, I was taken out of my cage and my cage searched even though I had NOTHING and WAS BUTT ASS NAKED! Then just around December of 2008, I was visited by another officer by the name of S.O. Woods. He had some say-so and was able to come up to my cage, instructing the officer sitting in front of my door to take a walk. S.O. Woods told me this lone night, as I'm still freezing my ass literally off, but ass naked that what's fixing to happen has nothing to do with me, and that he knows what I'm being placed through right now is bullshit. But what's coming has nothing to do with me. Not fully understanding what the hell he was talking about because I hadn't slept in God knows how long and freezing cold. I didn't really pay any mind to what he was saying.

After he left, what seemed only maybe thirty minutes, I had a shit ton of people at my cage door, asking me what the fuck S.O. Woods said to me. Freezing and pissed, I told them to fuck off. I was removed by force from the cage, after being gassed with chemical agents and a team ran in on me. Beaten and burning from the chemical agents, I was no longer cold.

I found out that after S.O. Woods came and spoke to me and told me what he did. he went out to the parking lot, got into his truck, opened his lockbox, and placed his gun into his mouth before blowing his brains out. I was the last person that he spoke to S.O. Woods' death would have a great impact on my state of mind in the following years. Though deep within my core, I knew what he said was true, I still doubted because even though everything started behind some down- right evil correctional offic rs, it was also my actions that caused more problems than results in a positive light.

During the year 2009, I found myself being transported to a Psych prison known as J-4 (Jester-4). This would come from being constantly shaken down every 15 min- utes, which turned into every 30 minutes for months on end. Mental health would be allowed to come and check on me every so often, but there was only so much intervention that security would allow them to get away with because Mental health knew what they were doing to me was unjustified and downright Cruel and Unusual Punishment.

What made everything so bad was that I was now the black sheep on Texas Death Row. Everyone was being told that I snitched, when in truth that was incorrect and it was O.I.G. (Office Inspector General) telling these lies and it was also other prisoners that were working with the Office Inspector General. Then there was the fact that the directors back then and the Senate Chairman John Whitmire had all four (4) crossover doors (doors leading to the other sections around the Pods), they had these doors sealed shut with duct tape. Yes, you read that correctly, they made ranking officers go and seal the doors closed with DUCT TAPE, so that NOBODY COULD USE THESE DOORS TO CROSS INTO THE SECTION ISOLATING ME FROM EVERY-ONE!

I would be housed in these conditions for years but after a few months of only being taken out of this cage butt ass naked for a shower. While being watched by said lieutenants or sergeants, as they were the only ones allowed to enter into the section to feed me, shower me, or shake me down; though I had nothing. I started "jacking" the run. This means that every time they pulled me out of that cage to search it, they knew I didn't have anything for them to shake down, because I was still butt-ass naked. I would come out and then I would either refuse to go back into the cage, thus forcing them to have what is called a "use of force" or I would actually sit my bare ass down and also force them to have a use of force. A use of force is when at any time they need to utilize chemical agents on my person, or they have to utilize the hand-held video camera and place leg irons on my legs and then carry me back into the cage. I was doing this EVERY TIME they pulled me out to do their bullshit searches. If I wasn't allowed to sleep, get mail, nor have any kind of visits, and was only being fed a fucking food loaf for over a year now. Then they would have to do paperwork and actual fucking work then fucking with which they knew was fucking WRONG!

After S. O. Woods, suicide by blowing his fucking brains out in the parking lot of the Polunsky Unit in Livingston, Texas. I would be informed that everyone that was on my approved visitation list had been placed on my Negative Visitation list. This was in January of 2009. It didn't matter that back when I was busted with said cell phone, after trying to do the right thing.

My mother and sister would be arrested and charged with a felony. Here are two women that NEVER had any record with the law, and now because they wanted to speak to their son and little brother who was sentenced to DEATH, they were being charged. The only thing they did for me was purchase a pre-paid calling card from stores so that I could have minutes on the cell phone I was using. At no time was I using this phone to cause anyone undue problems or making money. I was simply talking to my loved ones like everyone else. But this wasn't enough in the eyes of shitheads like John Whitmire and the Office Inspector General and the Directors of the Texas Department of Criminal Justice.

Not long after I was told in my butt-ass naked isolation that I was also not allowed visit from my mother & sister, I would be told that I was being charged with two felonies. One for contraband and the other for Terroristic Threats. I would be represented by this other fucking idiot of a lawyer from the Texas Defender Service's. This would cause me to slip further into a state of depression, because I could handle myself being in trouble, but I couldn't understand or fathom that I was now responsible for my loved ones being in trouble and having to spend a couple of hours and days in a jail here in Texas. It was the last straw in a way for my mind and heart to handle.

The only thing I could do to try and make things right for them and for myself, was to take a deal in the District Court of Judge Elizabeth Coker here in Livingston, Texas. In accepting a total of twenty 120) years on top of my sentence of death, my loved ones would get 10-years' probation and a fine o around $1,000.00 each and community service.

Only years later would any of us find out that what the Judge did was wrong and basically the state got away with another injustice. But what sat and continues to sit wrong with me is the fact that everyone else that was busted with cell phones in prison, I was the only one being given free-world charges and getting time. Everyone else that got busted, was given a disciplinary case and received ninety (90) days restriction, before receiving everything back, and nobody else lost their visitation.

So, now I'm being completely isolated in a cage butt-ass naked and being shook-down every thirty (30) minutes' instead of 15-minutes, being fed a food loaf which is a mixture of the food being served to the prisoner's but baked into a loaf that taste like shit, but is the only thing I would be fed for over two fucking years! I was being denied sleep and humane treatment and lawyer's that were aware of my situation and the injustice of it all, did NOTHING to help me or my loved ones.

These were lawyers from known Law Firms around the State of Texas, and even the few from TDS Texas Defender services who were told by their clients who were housed on Death Row. Nobody reached out and tried to get me better treatment, because they were all fucking scared of going against the State of Texas and in general the Texas Department of Criminal Justice.

Lawyers that have no sense of humane treatment because in truth all we are to them is another paycheck from the courts to represent us. Who in their right fucking mind would want another person to go through shit like this and could honestly just sit back and not do a single fucking thing when they knew what was going on with me was FUCKING WRONG!?!

Then, after years of being isolated, I would be moved to an even worse section for the mind of a human being to handle. I was also given a Minister Visit from a woman that is a Quaker in Austin, Texas named Mary.

The day was January 2nd, 2011, I was moved over one section into a cell on A-Section of the same Pod I had been on A-Pod, but this cage though like the one I just left, had an in-cell video-camera mounted right up in the corner after entering the cage. It could see everything in the cage and it had access for audio.

I was now being housed in 12-AA-14 cage on the section known simply as "DEATH WATCH". This section houses the men with a set execution date, meaning they no longer have any appeals going for them and they're in their last few months of life before being taken from their cages and driven to Huntsville, Texas and the Death Chamber at the Walls Unit. Now, my interaction would be with other's by yelling from cage to cage, but it would be only with men waiting to be killed by the state of Texas.

A cold-blooded murder, regardless of the fact that it's what each of us were sentenced to, Death is Death and no matter what you call it, someone will still be dead at the end of the day. But, when is it humane to walk a grown man to a room that has a cold gurney, and ask him to be a man and lay down after walking himself or herself to this place of killing, so that you may then have a doctor, who is now violating his/her own oath not to kill is now taking part in doing just that.

Just a little while after being moved into #14 cage on Death Watch, an escort team would come to get me, as I was being escorted to a Minister visit with this woman named Mary from Austin, Texas. During our visit together, she let me know that she had spoken with my mother on the telephone, and that my Auntie had last her battle with Breast cancer that very morning, January 2nd, 2011, (R. I. P. Donna Bird).

Being able to block my pain/emotions back then, we continued on with our two-hour visit. Talking and laughing and getting to know one another. Upon me return alter our visit to my cage on Death Watch even phone call home because we're allowed one if there is a death in our families.

Not only was I denied my request to call home, but found out my mother had also called here and made the request to let her son know about the death of her sister my Auntie. She too would be told no, but what pissed me off and struck me as cruel & unusual punishment, was that the Assistant Warden, Timothy Lester, who everyone here and about called "Little Hitler", came and told me personally, that he didn't care if my mother died and my whole family, I would NEVER GET A PHONE CALL HOME TO MY LOVED ONES UNTIL I WAS DEAD MYSELF!

Not having anything else to utilize as he is screaming this at me, I did the only thing that came to mind and spit directly into his face and told him FUCK YOU, DICKSUCKER!

Sadly, and no surprise I found myself being ran in on by a seven men, use of force team fully outfitted in their riot gear. Before they ran in though I was covered with chemical agents. All property (clothing, mattress, and sheets) were again taken from me for longer than ninety 190) days. This would be the start of my further acts of retaliation against those who kept me where they were, and vice versa.

Malik Al Mawt

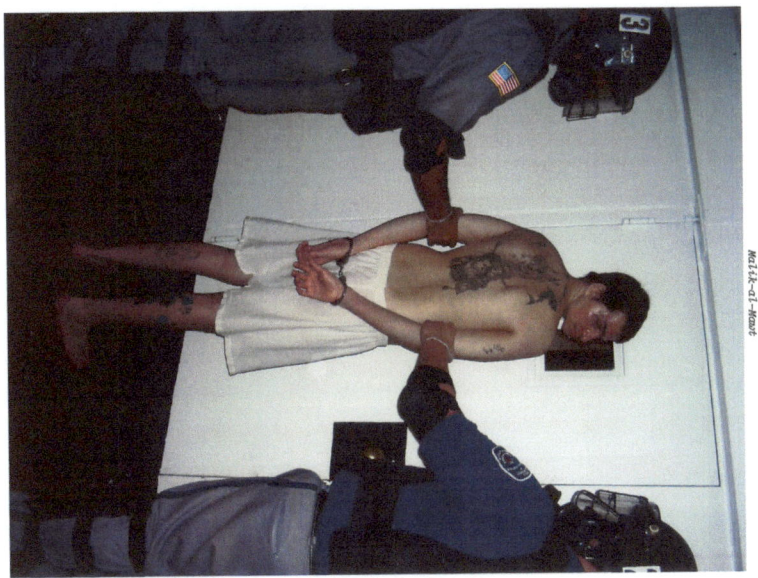
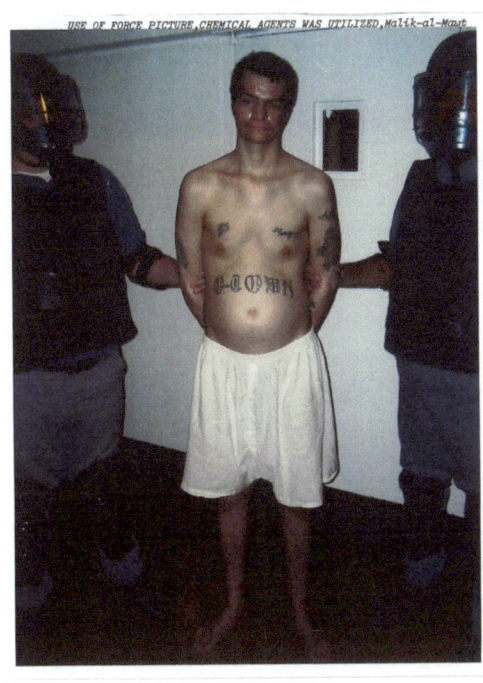

Malik Al Mawt

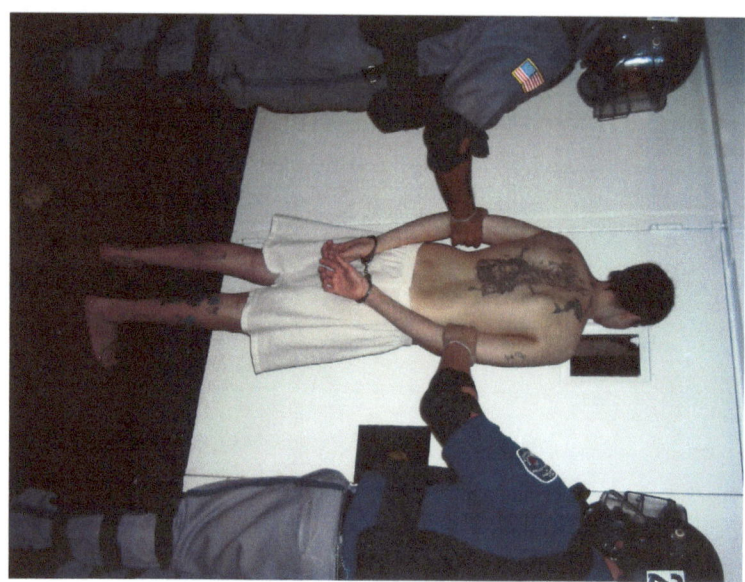

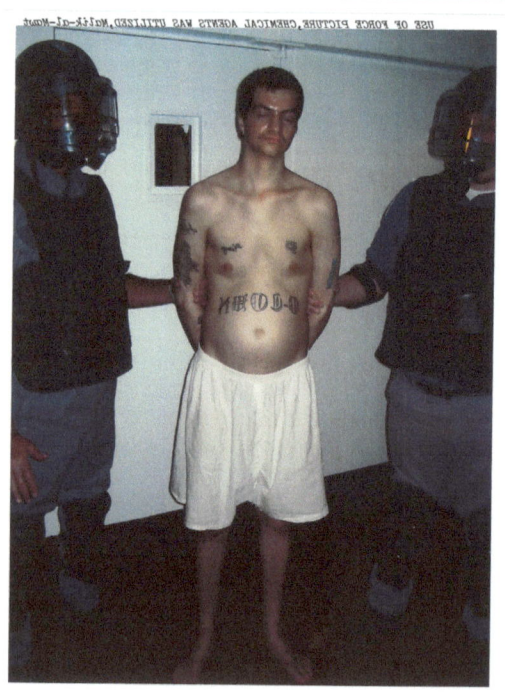

RICHARD TABLER

CHAPTER 2
"You're Not Forgotten"

The first couple of guys I ran back into for only the second time. Which would turn out to be my last, was "½ Deck" & "Tito" (Michael Hall, #999346 & Humberto Leal, #9991621. ½ Deck as everyone called him was housed in #4 cage down on one Row and "Tito" was directly under me in #7 cage. I never asked what they were locked up for because honestly, I didn't care at the time.

We were all sentenced to Death, and some of us would get there sooner than others, but it was the sole thing we each had in common. Death would become a part of our lives. One thing that neither of us could stand was the security light that was on 24/7 in the dayroom. This light would shine like it was pointed directly at our cage's and somehow would find its way directly into our faces as we tried to sleep. Though in truth, we knew this wasn't possible, it still felt like it.

So, one day when ½ Deck was in the dayroom, he and Tito & I got to talking about covering that fucking light up, seeing as we couldn't knock it out or break it cause, well that bastard sits about 20 or so feet above our heads. The only way to get at it would be to climb the dayroom bars and beat the shit out of it, but we knew this wouldn't work either. So, Tito shot a tube of Colgate Toothpaste to ½ Deck and I shot him some newspapers. We all agreed it would be best to just climb the bars, smear some Colgate over the light then place a few sheets of newspaper over the light, thus blocking it out.

For those of you shaking your heads, just stop. Tito brushed his teeth all the time, but glue was hard to get back here on Death Row from the idiots out in the General Population who would charge one of us an outrageous price for a fucking fin er of glue. A fin er for all you morons in society is a rubber gloves fin er chopped off then fil ed with glue, tied closed and sold to us idiots on Death Row. Tito's thinking was, why waste flags (Stamps) on such a fin er when Colgate works just as good if not better then glue?

So, up goes ½ Deck and next thing you know we have sheets of newspaper covering the dayroom secu- rity light. Nice and dim in the dayroom Now. After racking up, they did some showers (Correctional Officer s) and then it was lights out. The three of us slept great for a whole night.

The next morning, we were woken up by an officer in the dayroom with a long ass poll and a rubber scrapper on the end as he's trying to remove the fucking newspapers! Come on dude, we said, get your fat ass up the bars and take it down, you fucking want it bright in this bitch! The three of us yelled at this dude, man get the fuck out of here, that fucking light is too bright and we can't sleep with that shit on! No go, he managed to get most but not all of the newspaper off, that Colgate Toothpaste worked like a champ, because to this very day 12 years later it's still stuck up on that fucking light!

Sadly, ½ Deck was executed on February 15th, 2011, by the State of Texas. He was only 31 years old, and no doubt the man this fucking State is guilty of killing, wasn't the same man that was locked up many years before, because none of us are ever the same person we were twenty minutes later much less decades or more years later. (R. I. P. Michael Hall, #999346).

Between the heartless killing of our friend ½ Deck and the execution of Tito. Who also wasn't the same person he was when he was found guilty of Capital Murder. This is a man that taught myself and others how to braid key chains and little crosses and other necklaces and bracelets. He was also one hell of a cook! But you wouldn't know this because the state, let alone anyone in society wants you to know, how we as a whole on Texas Death Row are capable of changing, or becoming something better than the animals we once were.

Tito wash killed by the State of Texas on July 7th, 2011. (R. I.P. Humberto Leal, #999162). Not everyone that I would have to be housed around got along with me at first, one example is "Youngblood" (Milton Mathis, #999337). "Youngblood" as everyone knew him by, was at first pissed off at me, because like so many he believed what he was told, that I had snitched, but after some time I was able to prove to him that not only was this NOT true, but that others that he thought he knew were the ones in fact snitching. But before this happened, he called me every kind of name under the sun, from bitch to fucking piece of shit, to cracker and white boy, though these didn't bother me that much, they still pissed me off when added with the other names.

That's one thing prisoners are good at, name calling when one is stuck behind a steel fucking door. After a few months of being neighbors though, I was in the dayroom one day, when I heard him telling another inmate on the section that he had been trying to get a Rosary before his visit with his mother and other loved ones because though he cursed my ass out, he was catholic. He told his friend that he had asked the chaplain and even other prisoners but nobody had one and couldn't find on .

In all me time in prison, one thing I have come to realize and learn from just simple common sense is that, in prison when we go to sleep, we're able to close our eyes and not see anything, but one thing we can NEVER do is shut off our ears so that we don't hear anything. Unless of course you have some headphones on your ears and are blasting your cheap ass radio that these fuckers rip us off for. Then sure, you won't hear much, but where I first learned to do time in DVI in Tracy, California. This was Gladiator School. You are always, ALWAYS PAYING ATTENTION TO YOUR SURROUNDINGS!

In California you never wanted to be caught slipping by, your enemy's because it was a good way to get yourself killed by another prisoner. Here in Texas though, they don't understand this method or think nothing of it, because they believe they're too tough or too bad ass to wind themselves on the receiving end of a shank. Thus, when I was in the dayroom as "Youngblood" was speaking to his friend and explaining his situation in regard to the Rosary. I was able to send a "kite" (note) to someone I knew on the other side of this Pod.

While I was still in the dayroom my answer came back. Reading the kite that was sent back to me. I sat at the table in the dayroom and wrote out a short kite to "Youngblood" before they came to get him for his visit with his mother and other loved ones. After writing what I wanted to, I folded it up and slid it under his cage door from the dayroom. Calling his name as I climbed down. He said what bitch? Shaking my head, laughing on the inside at this childish shit, I said get that kite I just slid under your cage door and read it.

Doing as I said, he came to his door after opening it and reading what I wrote and placed inside. He looked down on me in the dayroom from his cage on 2-Row, then shaking his head walked away, soon after the escorting team came and got him for his visit.

A few hours later, he returned and I was still stuck in the fucking dayroom, because they had been having uses of Force's down the hall on other Pod's. Thus, they could not rack up or switch out rec. He came back and had this HUGE smile on his face and slid a kite to me in the dayroom, showing me a picture of him and his mom out in the visitation along with other loved ones. With tears pouring down his face, he said, "Blue, man, I apologize for cursing you out and calling you those names.

Out of everyone that said they were friend's or could get anything, you were the one that went and found me a Rosary, so that I could have it and pray and take pictures with my mom and loved ones. Thank you." Less than one month before Tito's execution, "Youngblood" was also killed by the State of Texas. (R.I.P. Milton Mathis, #999337). He was taken from this life on June 21st, 2011.

Over time, I would come to learn that every time someone was killed and, regardless of their standing in life at that time, with me or I with them, each senseless killing of these men, would drive my mind to the edge, because now I would slowly come to have an understanding of what soldier's suf- fer from with PTSD, only mine would become better known as Survivor's Guilt.

While I would like to write about those that have left this shithole and those that only saw it as doing their job, by placing on a correctional Officer's uniform, even though they went beyond a job description when they started writing bogus disciplinary cases or intentionally placing roaches or rocks into our food, thinking we wouldn't notice.

I would like to also name those men both enemy and friend alike that was ruthlessly taken from this place and made to walk after being dehumanized and degraded by a strip search in-front of women and men on their last day of life. I would like for you to meet them here within these few pages and look upon their names, like you would when visiting the war Memorial, and though in your eyes we're not being killed by battles of war, in truth we most certainly are. Because we are at War with the State of Texas and the Criminal Justice system and the courts and the District

Attorneys and Attorney Generals who deep down inside are no better than either one of us. They too are cold blooded killers, only they are allowed to kill with the consent and backing of nation/State. Protected by laws and loopholes, those in Office are allowed to decide another's fate in life.

The names you are about to read, are not, NOT the same men that were sentence to DEATH in the State of Texas, but men who were loved and cared about by others in society who understood, what it meant to lose a loved one who was cheated out of a fair life, because they didn't have money and stations in life like many of You. Unlike you, my mind won't allow me to forget the men I watched and got to know, walk away from the section on Texas Death Row called, "DEATH WATCH!!! "These are the men that continue to live in my memory.

Michael "½ Deck" Hall, #999346
Timothy Adams, #999448
Cary "Hillbilly" Kerr, #999449
Gayland Bradford, #996
Lee Taylor, #999344
Milton "Youngblood" Mathis, #999337
Humberto "Tito "Leal, #999162
Mark "Slayer" Stroman, #999409
Martin Robles, #999457
Steven Woods, #999427
Lawrence Brewer, #999327
Frank Garcia, #999418
Guadalupe Esparza, #999385
Rodrigo Hernandez, #999474
George Rivas, #999394.

One thing about Rivas was that even though he was a part of the Texas 7 that had escaped custody and was finally caught in Colorad . He wasn't a heartless killer like so many made him out to be. Rivas as he was known by his friends and enemies alike could fix just about anything that was broken and made with electronics. He would get someone's Radio and upon request and a little fee, he would then by-pass certain circuits within the circuit board and hook up TV on our Radio's so that we could listen to movies that came on out there in society such as USA, and TNT and CBS, ABC and numerous other TV stations.

I remember, one thing he taught me how to do, after becoming so pissed Off, at the officers atching me and everyone else on Death Watch, through the in-cage video cameras. Officers ould criticize and tell us to take something down in our cages because it was blocking their view into our cages. Finally having enough of this I asked "Rivas" what I could do if anything to knock-out the infrared? He told me to take some kind of reflector (i. . aluminum-foil. Basically, take a coffee bag and flip it inside-out). hen place this over the infrared part of the camera without blocking the actually camera itself. And leave my cage light on for a few minutes. After doing this, I would then block out my back window that allowed a sliver of light to come in but, wouldn't actually allow me to see outside other then C-Pod's walls directly. Once this was done, I would then turn out my cage light, then pull off the cover I had laid up on the infrared. For some crazy ass reason, I'll never understand, this would completely knock out the infrared and prevent officers from atching me in my cage at night or whenever I had it blacked out in my cage.

It was fucking hilarious, because I would be standing at my cage door talking to someone down the run. While also watching the officer in the control picket doing his or her best to try and stalk us on the video screen in the picket. When I would be standing there, then turn out my cage light and all of a sudden, I would disappear. One minute they could see me on camera and then the next they couldn't. I could see them watching the screen, when all of a sudden, you'd see their fucking heads snap up and around looking directly at my cage door, and back to the video-screen trying to understand why the fuck my cage would no longer show up on the video-screen! Like I said it was fucking hilarious! Without them fulling knowing what was going on, I must have knocked out and off-line fi e of those fucking cameras.

Keith "Thumper" Thurmond, #999435. Thumper as we all called him by his nickname, which was "Thumper". He was this stocky little white dude and a little over-weight from Montgomery, county. Back in 2012 there was this shithead of a major named Virgil McMullen. This piece of shit acted like he was top dog and that everyone would do as he ordered.

Two, incidents that took place with me with McMullen in 2012, and one of them would later involve "Thumper's" help. The first one as, this Unit (prison) was on it's annual lockdown. Officer as entering into each section with this orange crate that was maybe 3 feet X 3 feet X 2½ feet deep. We were told we had to place all our property into this fucking crate and what was not in it would be confiscated and or thrown into the trash. Legal work and other such property are NOT to enter into this crate, but that shithead Major McMullen was ordering his officers to confiscate l   al work that was left outside this crate. Needless to say, all of my legal work was not only confiscated, but thrown into the fucking garbage.

This was my life and could help me get off Death Row. Only later on would I be able to have it resent to me by lawyers, but it took some time doing so. The next time, I was out at a Minister visit with my friend Mary from Austin. When I was being escorted back onto the Pod and my section to my cage #14, other officers   ere in the process of removing all my personal property. When I asked them why, I was told that Major McMullen had ordered it, alongside him and backing his order up was the assistant warden back here at the time, Assistant Warden Ruiz.

After being placed into my now empty cage, a few min- utes passed before another escort team came to get me to take my down to the Major's offic . I told them that I was refusing and that he could go fuck himself. They left only to return with more officer . I was ordered to submit to a strip search, then ordered to place my hands behind my back out my food-slot so that restraints may be placed on Me. Doing so, I was then escorted out of my cage and placed directly into the shower still in handcuffs behind my back. My mattress was taken and thrown from 2-Row downstairs along with my sheets and blanket and toilet paper and state green soap, no bigger than a fucking chitlin gum. I was then taken from the shower and placed again into my cage. As soon as they removed the handcuffs, you could hear that Dick sucker McMullen over the Radio (walkie-talkie) to bring that inmate to his office n w.

Being fully pissed of now, I went because I had nothing else to do now. Getting down to the shithead's offic , I'm ordered to take a seat in the chair that was placed in front of his desk. Facing him, sitting behind the desk, I then take notice that assistant warden Ruiz is standing off to my right side, as when I entered, he was blocked from my sight because he was standing almost behind the office door when it   as opened.

Once seated, the assistant warden told the escorting team to leave and close the door behind them. After they left it was just the three of us. though he would remain out of most of the conversation, assistant warden Ruiz was no less guilty of being a dirty warden then McMullen was of being a fucking pussy. As Major McMullen is laughing at me, explaining that he could buck me over any time he wanted to and could get away with it. I interrupted him and told him sure; I understand why you're doing this now. And I even have compassion towards you, Major. I mean I would be pissed off at that world too if my mother named me some bitch ass name like Virgil, Virgil!

Before I knew it, he had gotten up red faced and walked around the desk and threw a left-hand punch that landed on the right side of my face and knocked me from the chair I was sitting in. Getting up, I could feel my face swelling from the hit, I had a split-second thought of coming out of my handcuffs and beating him with a stick from a hatrack that was laying on the floo . But, like I said it was split second and in that second, I knew it would be my word against theirs because there were no video-cameras inside the Offic . Assistant warden Ruiz opened the office door and the esco t team took me back to my cage on Death Watch.

As I was coming up the stains to 2-Row, I had to pass by "Thumper's" cage #12. Unbeknown to me he was standing at his door, so that when I was walking up the stairs, he could see the side of my face and head on the right. Once the officer s left, he hollered down to me and said, "Hey, Blue! What the fuck happened to your head and face dude?"

Because I had no property, I was unable to look at myself in the mirror, but "Thumper" saw right away that swelling and the bruising already taking place on my head and face from the suck- er-punch from Major Virgil McMullen. I told him what happened and what I said to him. Thumper said he's let his lawyers know when he went out for his legal visit later on that day.

One day later someone from the Office Inspector General came to speak with me after their office   as contacted by my shitty lawyers John Jasoda & David Schul- man, who were contacted by "Thumper's "lawyers and talked about the assault by the Major and Warden. One day after I spoke with O.I.G. (Office Inspector General). A Doctor came and took a polygraph test, though I would never be told the results, other than that they're office said Major McMullen ould never assault an inmate. Only years down the road would everyone come to find out about the disregard for justice, as he would be charged innumerous assault and abuse charges against prisoners throughout his time as a Major and even assistant warden, before being fired y the Texas Department of Criminal Justice.

That's how it works inside prison walls, though. If an officer is filed o for assault or has numerous disciplinary cases written against prisoners. TOCI-ID doesn't punish them, no by far they do the very opposite and promote them.

Jesse Hernandez, #999425
Beunka Adans, #999486
Yokamon Hearn, #999292
Marvin Wilson, #999098
Robert Harris, #999364
Cleve "Sarge" Foster, #999470
Jonathan Green, #999421
Bobby Hines, #999025
Donnie Roberts, Jr., #999487
Mario "Skinny" Swain, #999475.

"Skinny" as his friend's knew him, was this youngster from the West coast, and I remember this one time he and I had cooked a spread together (food/ taco's). I had him shoot his line Hishing line, is something we make or braid so that we can use this to pass books, food, ext. I to one another through the side of our doors or through the bottom back then, as the cage doors were not sealed up as they are today. So, as I told "Skinny" to shoot his line through the side of his door, I was able to pull his line through the side of my door, where I poured a can of coke into a chip bag, so that I could transport it to him in his cage. Once he got it, he started laughing as he told me this was the first time he ever got a coke in a bag!

Ramon Hernandez, #999431
Preston Hughes, #939
Carl "Big Buck" Blue, #999151
Ricky "Short Dog" Lewis, #999097
Ronnie Threadgill, #999424
Richard "Psycho" Cobb, #999467

Carroll "Tick" Parr, #999479
Jeffery Williams, #999350
Elroy Chester, #999280
John Quintanilla, #999491
Vaughn Ross, #999429
Douglas "Birdman" Feldman, #999326.

"Birdman" used to have the crazy bad habit of cutting someone's line if it passed directly in front of his cage when he didn't get along with someone. He also used to make these origami footballs and fin er-punt them outside his cage door so they covered the fucking floo .

Robert Garza, #999466
Arturo Diaz, #999345.

"Diaz" as he was known back here on the Row was a known gang member with the Pistolero's, but when I met him the first time, it was after being moved from F-Pod level-3 to B-Pod level-1. I was housed in #36 cage and he was in #42 cage with his other Pistolero, Carlos Trevino in #31.

Trevino was back then a huge fan of that kid's book Harry Potter, don't even get me started on that shit. Diaz though and Trevino shared with me on one of the numerous Mexican Holiday's, a spread of Taco's and a few bottles of Hooch. Diaz also was one hell of a speaker maker, if you provided the material for him to make one, he could hook you up a speaker for your cage. I had him make me one, with this Magnet I had that came from a visitation phone someone had given me. I used to play that thing on Friday nights and it sounded as if you were back in the clubs with friends.

The second time I met up with him it was when they moved him onto Death Watch, with an execution date for September, 26th, 2013. I'm not a big chess player but back then I would play every once in a while, "Diaz" bet me this onetime and ended up losing his chess Board to me, which was sent home to my loved ones after his execution.

Michael Yowell, #999334
Jamie "Lurch" Mccoskey, #999053.

"Lurch" was a truly and sincerely great fuck head! He couldn't stand up and walk and had to use a walker to go everywhere. When he wasn't getting into with someone else, he and I were getting into it. He would scream at me that I was a snitch and a bitch, and I would turn right back around and tell him, who are you calling snitch!?I have paperwork that show's you I didn't snitch mothafucker and who you calling a bitch, You're the BITCH motherfucker, can't even get up off your fucking knees! Bitchass motherfucker using a walker and talking shit when you know you just a fucking cell soldiering bitch ass! He left this life being a dicksucking ass bitch too.

Jerry Martin, #999552.

Jerry left out of here drunker than a fucking skunk. It was fucking hilarious because they had to help him down the stairs on his way out of here. But truth was Jerry didn't fight his appeals, because he was burdened with guilt for his crime which was an accident. He and another prisoner escaped from a prison in a stolen prison truck and an officer on horseback placed her horse in front of the truck and two prisoners' thinking they would stop. Instead, when they swerved to try and go around her, they clipped her horse which in turn threw her. The fall cost her her life and placed Jerry and another here on Texas Death Row.

Jerry used to be a really great artist and a lot of his work could be found at many other prison's on the walls and in the chow halls, but once he was found guilty of Capital Murder, all his stuff was painted over by others at the orders of prison staff. Jerry didn't set out to kill this officer when he and another escaped, it was pure accident, but in the end he paid for her life with his own life and did the only thing he knew how at the time. Give her family some kind of closure by ending his appeals and volunteering for execution. When he left this life he did so on his terms, and drunker then a skunk!

Edgar Tamayo, #999130
Ray Jasper, #999341
Anthony Doyle, #999478
Tommy Sells, #999367
Ramiro Hernandez, #999342
Jose Villegas, #999417
Willie "T-Rock"Trottie, #999085
Miguel "Pisa" Paredes, #999400.

"Pisa"also in English known as "Fatboy"was also an ex-gang member with the Pistolero's and was friend's with both "Diaz" and Carlos Trevino. One thing that stood out from "Fatboy" though was the talent he had in art. This dude was badass in a good way with either graphite or ink pen, and he could also cook. In fact while he was housed on Death Watch and before his execution, he and I had the chance to go outside to rec and speak to one another from our own rec yard cage.

During this conversation, he would explain to me how to make a "Cheese Cake" with a pint of Blue Bell Ice cream and some other things you had to purchase from the Unit (Prison) commissary. The first time I made one, and shared it with both "Fatboy" & another prisoner on Death Watch named "Prieto". I would become known to them as the "Baker" by "Fatboy". Because the Cheese cake I made one day was out of a Peach Cobbler Pint and was even better then, "Fatboy's"!

Arnold Prieto, #999149.

"Prieto" to his friends, was like "Fatboy" and many other's but maybe a touch better then them and most if I'm being honest. This dude was off the chain when it came to doing ink pen works of art. The only thing was, he was fucking color blind, like I am in one eye and he took for fucking EVER to do one drawing.
Robert Ladd, #999237

Donald "Lizard" Newbury, #999403.

"Lizard" to his friend's and also his enemy's was one of the Texas 7 that escaped only to be caught weeks later in Colorado along with "Rivas" and others. The thing about "Lizard was that if you fucked up and failed to follow policy, because offic rs were always screaming at us about policy when it suited them, but when we did some thing that was in their eyes not policy, they wrote disciplinary cases no matter what. This was a fuck ass move. so when they would fuck up and "Lizard "took offense or he was simply bored. He would black out his cage, and make Rank utilize a 7-Man Team Use of Major Force.

They would come on the Pod in their riot gear suited up and utilize chemical agents, as this didn't bother him or any of us so much as it did their own staff. You'd see and hear officers that weren't a part of the use of ForceTeam and didn't have a gasmask on coughing and walking around with snot hanging down their fucking faces.It was funny as fuck, because I would be standing there looking out the side of my cage door tell "Lizard" through the vent who was #1 Man and would be entering first all the way to the last man and what Rank was stand- ing outside his door and where.

I remember one such time, when he and I were on the outside rec yard, and he told me what he was plan- ning on doing that day. It was his Birthday. I racked up when they came to get me and told him have fun and that I'd be watching. When they went to get him off the yard he refused to rack up, thus Rank was notified and came down to find out what the problem was. "Lizard" told them it was his Birthday, suit that shit up! The Lieutenant that showed up was none other then LT. Raymond Newberry. The Major that showed up back then was Major Paul Tolley. They tried like crazy to get "Lizard" to come off the rec yard to no go. It just was NOT going to happen.

While a 7-Man Team was suiting up for war because they each knew this was going to get down right dirty if not painful, because "Lizard" had a history with them of fighti g, and when he was in the right and they the wrong on the few times. He would fight with weapons. This time though he wasn't doing that, he was just having some fun. A gas cannister was thrown into the yard and lit up the whole yard that we could see through the window into a huge white cloud before it turned dark reddish-orange and when it turned this color, oh my god did it smell fucking GREAT, (being a smartass, but you could smell the chemical agents. Officers are choking and I'm laughing, yelling aloud to him outside, "Lizard! Beat their fucking asses!) Next we heard the distigushed sounds of the paintball gun, "pop! pop! Pop!.. popopopopop!!! LT. Newberry is up on the roof trying to fire down into the rec yard on "Lizard" and not hitting a motherfucking thing, except the glass window a couple of times.

By this point though, nobody could even see outside onto the rec yard because the chemical agents were just simply that fucking strong and cloudy. Just before the 1-Man Team ran out onto the yard, Major Paul Tolley tried a gas can- nister one more time. Pulled the pin and threw it into the rec yard where he thought Lizard was standing. Only to find out just before the door to the outside rec yard closed all the way, for the very same fucking cannister to come flying right back inside, gassing everyone of us fuckers along with him and them!

That day was priceless and one to remember for the ages. But, "Lizard was able to show change within himself as well.

We all have days where we act out in some way or another or we take offense at what another says to us or even tries to do to us. But, one day that would shock all the Rank and even some in the Chaplaincy, was the day of his execution, which was the day be- fore my 36th Birthday. "Lizard" was going to be on a special transport that day. Meaning that instead of getting his last ½ day of visitation from 8:00am- Noon before being placed on a Van to transport him to the walls Unit in Huntsville, Texas. He was going directly from the dayroom that very morning of February 4th, 2015. While he was in the dayroom, unbeknown to him and I. There was a 7-Man Team suited up standing in the hallway right off the Pod, waiting to come and get him.

Everyone was expecting him to fight and they knew it would be more or less to the death. However, while my friend was in the dayroom, he asked me, "Blue, What should I do?" I looked down at him from my cage in #14 like he was crazy. "What the fuck do you mean, what should you do? Why the fuck you asking me? Seriously ,what do you think I should do?" I, said. "Lizard, don't give these fuckers what they want. Just walk like a man the whole way, regardless of the shit they try to say. If you do this, I'll fade the Team, whatever you want."

His response stunned me. "Blue, I'll do that and I will give you my word, if you give me your word, you won't fade the Team nor get any more disciplinary cases while you're here." I told him he had my word. Not twenty minutes later they came and got him and took him to Huntsville to be executed.

A couple of days after his execution, I was approached by the Unit Chaplain and other Ranking Officers, who told me that they had a message for me from "Lizard". I looked at them and asked what did he say? They told me that he asked them to tell me that he kept his word, and walked from the time they came to get him even though they were screwing him over on visits. He walked to the van and when he got off it, into the holding cage a few doors down from the Death Chamber. Then he walked and laid on the gurney and allowed them to bill him. They then thanked me for asking him to walk, because EVERYONE was expecting him to fight, that's why they were transporting him earlier then normal. Rest in Peace my friend.

Manuel Vasquez, #999336.

"MeMe" to his friends was also Mexican Mafia. He was good at making things in his cage such as watch bands and other items, and he loved playing chess with those around him here. I remember one time I and another prisoner who got a life sentence named Dauane Buck, were on a medical transport to go the Hospital down south. When they came and got the two of us around 4:00am we were shackled up tighter then Fort Knoxs before escorted to a Van. Thinking he and I would be in this van to the Hospital, we were stunned to be driven to another prison in Huntville, before both he and I were placed onto a Bus with a shitload of other prisoner's. Upon stepping up into the Bus and being chained to another prisoner I had never set eyes on before. It wouldn't be for many other's in that bus having never seen me before.

On the ride to the Hospital, I could see the Mexican I was chained to looking at me, from the side, as I was watching the cars and trucks on the freeway. Thinking that this dude know's who I am and saw me on the News from when I was the cause of a system wide lockdown back then for contraband. I started working my restraints and unlocking the box that trapped my handcuffs, so that I could remove them to defend myself. Just when I felt it would happen any second, the dude surprised me. "Hey, man! Ain't you that dude that caused the system wide lockdown for calling that State Senator?"

As I felt my body tense up, I turned to the dude and said yeah, that's me, what of it? Dude looked at me for a long second all serious like, before busting out laughing and telling me, that shit was funny as fuck dude. All the Homies were fucking laughing back at Ellis, because we wanted to kill that fucker you called. Man dude, tell my cousin when you get back to Death Row I said what's up! I said who's your cousin? He told me "MeMe" (Mexican Mafia, Manuel Vasquez). I said What's your name? He told me they call him "Maddog" and "MeMe" is his cousin and also his captain in the Mexican Mafia. We shook hands and chopped it up, just before getting back into Hunstville and being loaded onto a Van, I was told that if I ever needed anything to get word to him and it would be done.

Kent Sprouse, #999471
Manuel Garza, #999434
Derrick Charles, #999451

Lester Bower, #764
Gregory Russeau, #999430
Daniel Lopez, #999555
Juan "Homicide" Garcia, #999360
Licho Escamilla, #999432
Raphael Holiday, #999419
Richard Masterson, #999414
James Freeman, #999539
Gustavo Garcia, #999018
Coy Westbrook, #999281
Adam Ward, #999525.

"Ward" to those who knew him was a one-of-a-kind piece of shit to the very end. He acted tough but was NOT. He would curse you and shit you down and scream at you, but he was still a piece of shit. Back when I was housed on B- Pod and was involved in the taco and hooch spread with "Diaz"& "Trevino". I was in the shower which is directly in front of the dayroom and vice versa.

That day I was in the shower "Ward" was in the dayroom and gad climbed up on the bars to 2-Row talking shit to me in the shower. "Diaz" was telling me, "Blue, man don't pay no attention to that punk. We got food and drink in a few when you get back to the cage". Trying to do just that and mind my own business in the fucking shower mind you. This bitch "Ward" just would not give up and climbed back up the bars to take another stab at his verbalness, before he got the shock of his life not realizing that the whole fucking time he's been screaming his bullshit at me, what he didn't know but "Diaz"did was that I had opened the shower door, and was holding it.

Thus, giving in to my darker side, when "Ward" climbed back up to 2-Row to curse me out and talk shit about my Mama. I came out the shower and pushed his ass off the bars! Have you ever seen a body come flying down from somewhere high up, knowing that it shouldn't be flyin down like that? Let me tell you, that whole section got mute. It was like a slow-motion picture as you see this bitch flying backwards off the bars, I mean what kind of fuck- ing idiot jumps off the bars like that from twenty + feet up, only to land on concrete below? I mean I came out of that fucking shower so fast and stepped right back in, nobody other then "Diaz" knew I came out of it and pushed this bitch off them bars. Sure, he was fucked up, but by the time officers got around to racking him up or trying to get him to come and cuff up from his lying down where his bitch ass fell, I was already back in my cage and eating taco's and drinking hooch. But now that "Ward" was being moved onto Death Watch because he now had an execution date. That old saying what comes around goes around, couldn't have been more true, as I was in the dayroom when he came onto the Pod and attempted to spit into my face but missed and hit the officer escorting him in. But let me tell you he came real fucking close!

Pablo Vasquez, #999297
Barney Fuller, #999481
Christopher "Cujo" Wilkens, #999533
Terry Edwards, #999463
Rolando Ruiz, #999145 James Bigby, #997
Tai' Chin "Big Tai" Prey or, #999494.

"Big Tai" to his friend's and family alike was truly a one-of-a-kind person. I had first met "Big Tai" when I first rolled up to this shithole of a Unit in 2007 and was housed on F-Pod, level-3. Out of all the men that would come across my path since being on Texas Death Row, and then Death Watch.

"Big Tai" by far was the one to truly show a change from within. He had this heart, that maybe at one point in time had shown some vengence, but by the time I entered into his like and he mine as friend's who would become like Brother's. "Big Tai" showed only compassion for others.

Whenever we were housed on the same Pod, which wasn't very often, because I would be isolated from the normal part of Texas Death Row, before being moved to Death Watch. We would go outside and play games of "Run & Shoot". This is a basketball game where we're each on our own court (caged yard) and would start from one side and start shooting the ball into the net, once you made a shot, that counted as 1. You'd then run to the opposite side and shoot from there. The object of the game was to score 10 points before the other person did. Most time's game's would be close and at time's when you were both neck and neck, the rule was you had to win by 2 points.

"Big Tai" & I would play this game non-stop rain or shine, sweating our asses off. We'd play anywhere from ten games to fifty games of 10 points. Other days we'd just shoot the shit and talk about family and things we did out there in society, before fucking our lives up and ending up here on Texas Death Row. Other times, we would study the Holy Bible and the Holy Qu'ran at the same time. This was because "Big Tai" was a Five Precenter and because at one point in my own life I had studied the Holy Qu'ran when I was gang affiliated out in California and down in Florida, with "Kumi Nations".

The things that stood out about "Big Tai" was that he loved to cook and eat anyone of the cheese cakes I would make! He also thought he was Mr. Badass at Battle Ship and Hangman, which the two of us played all the time and even had offi- cer's taking our moves to other Pod's to each other.

Then one day just before the month of his own execution, he would save another pris- oner's life here on Texas Death Row, from dying by my own hands. Throughout many years after his heartless murder by the state of Texas. I would wonder why he had me let this dicksucker and known child molester live, when in my opinion he deserved nothing but a slow and painful death.

Steven Long, has no idea just how lucky he was the day I had him in a choke hold from inside the dayroom, before the voice of "Big Tai" broke through my rage. I understand why he had me let him go, even though when I think back to that day, I still don't agree with it. Because how can you justify saving the life of a known child molester that has no remorse for his actions, over that of someone that shows remorse for his actions and has taken the time while inside prison to better himself and help others in need?

"Big Tai" was taken from his loved ones lives and those that knew him here way too soon. I understand that we all are scheduled to die at one point in our lives, and in truth I'm okay with that as I know death is a part of life, but where some deserve to be executed, there are some who should not be killed, because they have shown that change is possible. May you Rest in Peace, "Big Tai".

Robert "Tool" Pruett, #999411
Ruben Cardenas, #999275
Anthony "T-Bone "Shore, #999488.

"T-Bone" as everyone knew him was an artist and a serial killer, who could have had the chance to work with police to give up the bodies of others, but instead went out like an evil creature to the end.

William "Old School" Rayford, #999371
John "Batman" Battagila, #999412

"Batman" to those who knew him, was a heartless sumbitch, to the end. If you didn't agree with him on something, then he would call you every name in the book, and yet this is a man that to get even with his wife, murdered his children while she was on the telephone with him.

There are some to this day who still thinks highly of this piece of shit, but I'm not one of them and though I tried to help him and show some kind of kindness to him at the end, it wasn't by my own strength that I did so. Anyone and I mean ANYONE who murders children should be put to death either right away or slowly by those the child was taken from, period. To show such a person compassion after killing some kids, it makes me wonder what kind of country would allow this.

Rosendo Rodriguez, III, #999534
Erick Davila, #999545
Juan Castillo, #999502
Danny Bible, #999455.

"Speedy" to his friend's and I first met when they brought him in his wheelchair down to F-Pod level-3. He was this old white guy that sued TDCI and won after they were in an accident. However, ever since he was left wheelchair bound and on Death Row. When I asked him what the fuck he was doing down here on level-3 with us, he told me that he had chunked on Stephen Barbee, but not shit .He chunked his chocolate syrup on his bitch ass for talking shit to him.I laughed my ass off at this because Stephen Barbee was a shit talker and could only get around by using a walker and crawling on his knee's.

One thing that really stands out to me about "Speedy" to this day is, when he was down there on F-Pod with us other killers. Officer s would have to come and get him on nightshift and take him to the medical shower. This one night this one officer named Claudette Lee came to get him, and as she's wheeling him back from his shower in his wheelchair, she just about kills the bastard after running his wheelchair into the fucking crash gate to enter into the section, thus about spilling "Speedy" from his chair. To this day, I still give officer Lee shit about her drving skills.

One thing about Officer lee is she's a dedicated office and is willing to work, but she's not one to fuck anyone over, regardless if it's an officer or prisoner. I have seen her leave this place and try her hand at being a police office , only to return and become a Lieutenant, then to give it up and work as a simple offic r. One thing she's got going for her too, is a smoking hit body and a matching attitude. My hat if I had one, is off to you, Officer . Lee!

Christopher Young, #999508
Troy Clark, #999351.

"Pennywise" to his friend's. This dude takes the cake for being down to earth and funny as shit, and willing to help out others regardless of who they are or what they did. Unless you directly fucked him over, he would give you the shirt off his back, though he was def as fuck, "Pennywise" was funny as shit. Rest in Peace my friend.

Daniel Acker, #999381
Robert Ramos, #999062
Joseph Garcia, #999441 A
lvin Braziel, Jr., #999393
Robert Jennings, #956
Billie Coble, #976
John King, #999295.

"Possum" to those who know him, was the smut king of Death Row. If you wanted pictures of bitches and bitches showing you their pussy lips spread wide open or fuck shots of women getting fucked by numerous men, taking dicks into their mouths, asses and pussy's at the same time, "Possum" was the man to see. He had some in the mailroom doing whatever he wanted, this was because deep down even though some in the mailroom act like they're offended at such picture's, they in fact enjoyed them and got off at looking at the picture's "Possum" had coming in through the mailroom, or any pictures anyone else had coming in.

Though his crime was fucked up. He and others dragged a Black man in Jasper, county Texas with their truck, he would come to turn his life around and pretty much stayed to himself and his select group of friend's.

But, like I said he loved him some pussy shot and I cannot blame him, because I and many others here love some pussy, though we cannot get it, that doesn't stop us from getting books and reading about it or enjoying a Penthouse Letters book. Most guys would catch a masturbation case within these walls for jacking thier dicks off on the female officers. Thus being served what TDCI calls a Code-20 case. I have not only NEVER DONE THIS. You couldn't pay me enough to even think about jacking my dick on one of these bitches, because by god a dog looks better than more then half these beast. And the very select few I do find attractive, I keep it to myself unless they approach me.

In twenty 1201 years of lockup I have never caught a Code-20, because I just don't do that kind of shit. Like I said, these beast are not something to be looking at, half the time, they are having incest anyhow. Thanks, but no thanks, I'll stick to my imagination, my hand or books or picture's if I really need them.

Larry Swearingen, #999361
Billy Crustinger, #999459
Mark Soliz, #999571
Robert Sparks, #999542.

"Sparks" as he was known, is the only prisoner I watched as they came to get him, rolled his cage door open on Death Watch the day of his execution, without cuffing him up, because he was in the process of taking his own like in an attempt to cheat these bastards out of doing it. Sadly, he was unable to do the deed, and ended up fight ng his way out to the end, but I gave him credit for trying.

Justen Hall, #999497
Travis Runnels, #999505
John Gardner, #999516
Abel Ochoa, #999450.

(Abel to those who knew him) was one of a kind and though he too had a fucked up case. I came to like being around him, because he truly was a changed man and was living his life to the end for God and always blessing those around him. Officer and Inmate ali e. He would call down to you or someone else and be like, "Blue, do you know what time it is?" and he'd say it's coffee Time, coffee Time, Blue. Have a Blessed day my friend!" He always had a kind word for each person he came into contact with. Rest in Peace, Abel.

Billy "Bandit" Wardlow, #999137
Quintin "G2" Jones, #999379
John Hummel, #999567
Rick Rhoades, #999049.

"Rick" to his friends, left out of this fucking place higher then a bite. This one day he got his hands on some meth and was found throwing all his personal property outside his cage door soaking wet from trying to flush it d wn the toilet first. He as seen by officer s making a Fort in his cage from his sheets, dude was a solid guy but when. some fucking idiot talked him into trying some meth, he was fucked up.

Carl Buntion, #993
Kosol Chanthakoummane, #999529.

(Kosolto his friends) This dude though we would have our fair shares of falling outs over time, was fucking awsome with that ink pen and his art work.

John Ramirez, #999544.

"Rambo" to his friend's and those who know him, was a shit talker, but in a friendly way if there is such a thing. He was also an artist and made things with his hands, though he was at one point in his life a Marine, nobody could understand why he wanted to be called "Rambo", when Rambo was inthe Army! I and others used to give him shit about this, but in the end he left walking like a man.

Tracy Beatty, #999484.

(Tray to myself and many others who knew him), Blew the minds of many on the day he was taken out of here to be executed in a senseless fashion. "Tray" use to be known for cursing everyone out and screaming at things and people that were not there. He had a skin condition that many failed to understand, but what happened when he was stuck on Death Watch between myself and Billy Tracy, was nothing short of amazing. He had cataracts and couldn't see worth a shit.so when mail came for him either Billy or I would read him his mail. I ended up helping him get his cataracts taken care of and got him approved for an audio watch and audio Bible. These few things changed "Tray"

Though I still write his wife to this day, she is harder in her ways, and some days I feel like throwing in the towel, but she's a friend and I care about her well being. "Tray" was Baptized three days before his murder and he was also married to a much younger woman his wire I write before he too left this life. What stood out the most when he left this place, was that he was singing the song "Amaz- ing Grace" and he could see with both of his eyes! Rest in Peace, my friend and buddy, Tray!

Stephen Barbee, #999507
Robert Fratta, #999189
Wesley Ruiz, #999536
John Balentine, #999315 Gary Green.#999561
Arthur "AJ" Brown, #999110

During the previous pages, you read about the guy's that I knew or was friends with. You read about their deaths and the things they & I did, and how we looked out for each other, ect... What you cannot know, and will never read about until the day I'm no longer among the living, is the pain and heartache I felt and continue to feel from their executions. You cannot fully understand how badly my having to watch those men leave that section, knowing full well that they were leaving to be killed. Just what that did to me mentally. It straight out fucked my head up, and caused me at many times, to try and take my own life.

When I wasn't trying to or thinking about ending my life, I was cutting on myself, but not in the sense that I wanted attention or to die, but in the sense that I was so pissed off, I wanted to cause pain to the officers and even other prisoner's that thought the shit was funny Ithe executions). Causing harm to myself was like hitting a reset button within myself, when I saw my own blood, I would calm down. If that's not some fucked up thinking, then what is.To this very day, I still suffer from nightmares that wake me from a dead sleep, and what's worse is I'm no longer housed on Death Watch.

I was moved on March, 21st, 2023 from "Death Watch" to F-Section on the same Pod, but into #76 cage. I was moved in part to the Lawsuit my lawyers of Killmer, Lane, & Newman, LIP. Filed on my behalf back in 2020 after retaining their services on October 3rd, 2018, and in part from then Warden D. Dickerson, who went out of his way, not for the first time, but many times on my behalf. So, once I was moved which took place on nightshift of the 21st of March 2023.

It took me days to clean the cage up that I was moved into, but what took place not even twenty-four hours after being moved, is what I want to bring to your attention. Simply put, I was Retaliated against and continue to be placed on Restrictions and I and my loved ones being punished without cause, nor charge nor disciplinary cases against me .

What is taking place against me is nothing short of that dicksucker John Whitmire abusing his place of authority as a senate Chairman, to come after me and attack me. And, if we're being honest, in my own opinion it's by far the stupidest decision this moron could have ever made in his life. What kind of idiot would knowingly chase after a convicted killer of capital Murder, after so many years of telling the public and those in L.E.O. |Law Enforcement Offices) that you FEARED for your life from me all those years ago. Then, and only after being housed and treated by correctional Officers with Cruel & Unusual Punishment and further isolated at your pathet- ic orders to 0. I. G. (Office Inspector General). You would now, only after I have shown that change was better and possible for myself. Only after I earned back my Visitation with my loved ones (ie. mother & sister) after 15 fucking years of NOT BEING ALLOWED TO VISIT THEM, you would knowingly and blatantly come after me and mine!? Was not the FEAR of GOD placed into your life a few years ago, when your Houston, Texas offic was shot up in what many called a drive-by of the office next door to yours. But think you stupid fool, why would anyone want to shoot up an office that sits next to yours that makes no money and has no ties to anyone or anything.

Now, and only after I've earned things back and worked for change in my life in a positive way, and have published my first to come of many nonfiction books. Now, you so boldly and openly come after me and again showing that you "think" you'll be able to get away with abusing your place of authority, in order to Retaliate against me and mine, without payment. On March 22nd, 2023. I'm escorted from my cage in #76 down to see then, Assistant Warden A. Enriques, who is the warden over Death Row 112- Building).

I'm escorted down to speak with this man, who starts questioning me about my first book that was published in 2021. I'm asked, how I came to write this book "Within The Shadows of Life". How much money am I making off of it, why did I write it, ect...To each answer I answered truthfully to Asst. Warden A. Enrriques. I even remember that it was a little after 6:00pm and he was waiting to go home and eat dinner, but had to stay late to question me because of this fucking dirtbag John Whitmire, who sent an email to Director's Brian Collier & Deputy Director Eric Guerrero. Until that time I had remained off everyone's radar, but now years later and ONLY AFTER I HAVE BEEN MOVED OFF OF DEATH WATCH, does John Whitmire come after me with his indirect questions. When in truth it's none of your fucking business!

After ten or fifteen minutes of answering questions, I'm then returned to my cage at a little after 6:20 pm. Only to get back to cleaning up this cage for living in, be- cause, it leaked rainwater like a floode dam. getting to sleep late into the night of March 22nd, 2023.

I'm again interrupted the next morning by two Sergeants standing at my door, telling me, "Tabler, come on, the Warden's want to speak with you "Getting up and out of my bed and then making them wait as I made my bed, brushed my teeth and washed my face, before giving them my boxers and other clothing to search, before getting dressed and placing my hands behind my back through my food-slat, to be handcuffed. I'm then escorted down to the Major's offic , where none other then, warden D. Dickerson, Asst. Warden A. Enriques, and Mr. Duff is waiting for me.

After I take a seat in the only remaining chair, the escorting, two sergeants, are asked to step outside and close the door behind them. This little gathering was something that they nor I wanted to happen. I was told that certain people were now placing pressure on the Administration of this Unit (Prison) , behind the Publishing of my first book and my being moved off of Death Watch.

I took the initiative to put the name of the person causing this bullshit out there, and though they were unable to directly share with me "who", it was shown by each of their reactions that I hit the nail on the head, senate Chairman & TDCI-ID Board Member, John Whitmire, was the sole person screaming like a fucking child who is no longer getting his way. This bitch is upset that I was not only moved, but that I was allowed to publish a book first of many. so, now he was going to make his actions against me known.

By blatantly and indirectly coming after me with having others do his dirty work for him, just as he did it back in 2008. I was told on that day of March 23nd, 2023" that sooner or later this would all blow over, but they had wanted me to understand that these questions were NOT coming from them.

I will not share which individual told me so, but I was advised to follow through with a Federal Lawsuit, because nobody at this Unit (Prison wanted any part of what they & I knew was going to follow Johnny boy, you fucked up this time, in coming after me, when you should have left me the fuck alone. Now if it's the last fucking thing I ever do in my life, I'm going to do every, and I mean EVERY FUCKING THING I CAN, EVERY FUCKING CONNECTION I HAVE, I AM GOING TO TAKE YOU FUCKING DOWN!! Oh, you misunderstand me, John Whitmire, I'm not going to harm a hair on your head, even though it's tempting to do so, no. I'm no longer in the business of killing in the physical sense, but your life of business. I'm going to utilize EVERYTHING, to end you legally.

A little over one week later, I and everyone else on Texas Death Row, got the telephone app on our Tablet's. Once our loved ones and friend's registered their own phone numbers with and through the Texas Phone System and securus Tech- nologies. We would be able to call from 2:00pm to 8:00pm Monday through Sunday, those people on are approved visitation list, only. These approved people along with their phone numbers would be in our electronic records and would be the only ones accessible through our Tablet's. You could get on your Tablet and call anyone, because it wouldn't let you. Your Tablet was being monitored and the time's you managed to get through on that piece of shit to someone on your visitation list, you were being recorded every second you were on the phone app. Securus Technologies and the Texas Department of Criminal Justice agreed that those of us who were Classified on Texas Death Row (Level-1 would have access to numerous apps on our Tablet and as long as we held a D1 level we would be allowed to utilize our phone app and the other apps on our Tablet, such as Messaging, Law Library, Pando, ect...) At no time has anyone of us nor myself had access to the Podcast, Movies, TV Shows, Live Streaming Radio, News Papers, Magazine's, Games. We were and are only allowed a selected few things, because of assholes like John Whitmire and his own personal ass licker Deputy Director Eric Guerrero.

On April 5th, 2023. Not even one week after speaking with the Warden's and Mr. Duff, I was again escorted down to speak with Asst. Warden A. Enriques, under a false guise, that he wanted to speak with me about my art supplies that had come in from an order placed to Dick Blick Arts. Only after I had been seated in the Major's office where Asst. Warden A. Enrriques was sitting and Captain N. Neyland was standing to the side, was I informed that as we sat there talking. His officers were inside my cage shaking me down and confiscating my Tablet. When I asked him why, he beat around the bush and said he couldn't tell me at that time, but I was NOT being downgraded nor was I being issued any kind of disciplinary case (he couldn't have done so anyhow, cause I broke no policy or rules). After being returned to my cage and seeing that my Tablet was indeed removed from my cage. I sat down on my bunk frustrated at this injustice being done against me, by John Whitmire and the Director's he was involving in his bullshit. Less then 12-hours later my Tablet would be returned to me by none other then Asst.Warden A. Enriques himself along with Mr. Duff.

Only after they had secured my food-slot, did they share with me that my OTS 106fender Telephone System had been removed. I already knew that they did something to it, or I should say had someone from se- curus Technologies remove the phone app. from my Tablet. Thus placing me on restrictions even though I was still a D1 and had not broken any rules or policy's.

It was now, April 7th, 2023.I never got the chance to speak with my loved ones on the phone app from my Tablet like every other Death Row prisoner was allowed to do, before they removed this phone app from my Tablet without cause. 60 days later to the date of April 7th 2023, my Securus Technologies account and Tablet was electronically closed/ shutdown. One minute I was tapping out a message to my family and the next not only was I locked out, but my Tablet was now showing it to be registered to another prisoner who was out in General Population.

It would take a week to speak to someone about this and, then it would take a few more days for them to turn my account back on and, that was when I noticed that all of my pictures had been deleted, I could no longer send instant Messaging to family, friends and lawyers, now my messaging was being held up for hours and even days and weeks before being sent or forwarded to my tablet.

Even as I sit here typing out this to you, my loved ones are suffering from health issues that keeps them from being able to travel from another State to visit with me, and yet I cannot call them directly from my Tablet like everyone else on Texas Death Row, even though I'm still a D1. Senate Chairman John Whitmire and Deputy Director Eric Guererro are doing everything that they can possibly get away with in fucking me over, even though they're doing so is an injustice.

During the month of July we were given maybe less then one week's notice that all our incoming mail would no longer be allowed snail mail. Instead it would now be sent by our family, friends and others to a processing center in Dallas, Texas. This everyone was being told was to slow the intake of "Dangerous Contraband" from entering into the prison's of the Texas Department of criminal Justice. We were given this notice by Director Timothy Fritzpatrick who is over classification and records of TDCI-ID. We would also be told this again in September of 2023 by Director Brian collier on the 7th. He would state more or less the same thing, but with a twist that now every prison throughout TOCI-ID would now be going to Digital Mail. This in their words was to prevent drugs and other contraband from entering into the prisons. This came directly after the State locked down all of their prisons throughout the State of Texas on a system wide lockdown to crack down on dangerous contraband. But, get this, what these Directors and others such as John Whitmire, are not sharing with you, is the cold blooded cover-up of a murder that took place here at the Polunsky Unit in Livingston, Texas.

A murder that could have been prevented had proper action been taken. Instead, they use the excuse of the 16 so-called homicide's they've had this year alone throughout the State. What they don't share with you is that sure, when someone dies it's called a homicide and is investigated by O.I.G. (Office Inspector General) and other L.E.O.'s (Law Enforcement Office s). But they don't share with you that most of these are not heartless murders, but suicide's, and or deaths of natural causes. thing you have been hear- ing on the Radio and on the TV's out there in society on the News Stations, are about the escapee from Chester, PA. The convicted killer Cavalcante, and how he's been on the run for over two weeks now. You hear about the escapee from the hospital in Washington, DC that got away with his handcuffs still on one of his arms. And you hear only once about Texas prison's being faced on a system wide lockdown. It's what you're NOT HEARING, that you should be.

It's the cover up by the Texas Department of Criminal Justice and Senate

Chairman and TDCJ-ID Board Member, John Whitmine. The heartless murder of one inmate out in the General Population by the hand of his cellmate.

You're not hearing the TRUTH and the FACTS of how the Directors allowed a Murder to happen and how a new Warden that has been here less then four months, along. with a new Major, have disregarded the ways of the previous warden's, only to now have General Population prisoner's killing one another and very recently one inmate "Bitch Slapping"a female officer on 4-Building, because she was running off at the mouth and being disrespectful to a prisoner. Turn the pages to read about this and so much more!!!

RICHARD TABLER

CHAPTER 3
"Cover Up"

On August 30th, 2023, two prisoners were housed together out in the General Population on the Polunsky Unit located in Livingston, Texas. For whatever reasons the Texas Department of Criminal Justice housed a violent inmate with a short timer who had under three years, with only one month left to go, before he would go home to his wife and family. These two inmates were housed on 8-Building's L-Pod, #2 cage.

On this pacifi day though the one inmate who gave officers an Inmate Request Form (I-60). Explaining that he FEARED for his life and that his cellmate was going to kill him. He needed to be moved. This took place on Wednesday, August 30th, 2023.

From the moment a correctional Officer was given this notice by the short timer inmate, a total of 72-hours and some change would pass. Along with a total of six 16) correctional Officers of the Polunsky Unit and it's newest war- den, Warden Ronald S. Ivey, and Major Vannessa Ward. These officers would not only lie about their doing a proper security check between the days of August 30th, 2023 & September 2nd, 2023, but would continue to lie when they were later questioned during the investigation that would follow.

Only one correctional Officer would be fired behind what I'm fixing to share with you. His firing was uncalled for as he not only admitted he fucked up, but he was also the only one out of six to tell the truth. The truth within these walls, is not looked upon as doing the right thing so that it would later be prevented from happening again. The truth here gets you fired while lying saves your job and the chance for other senseless murders to take place inside the prisons of the Texas Department of

Criminal Justice. On September 2nd, 2023 on 8-Building's L- Pod, #2 cage just before shift-change an officer mak- ing a proper security check discovered that one of the inmate's in this cage had been brutally murdered by his cellmate. He was found tied hand and foot like some kind of animal and was tortured to death. His face was badly beaten, his body was stabbed multiple times with a shank, his cock was damn near chopped off along with his feet. He was also burned. When his corpse was brought into 10-Building where Medical is located, the smell was so bad of a coppery smell along with the smell of a dead body, it caused those in turn-out for the shift coming on (night) to gag and for all in medical to try and flee from the smell.

During the coming Investigation by the Office Inspector General or I should say lack of Investigation. We find out that six officers lied about doing proper security checks, though video footage shows, that not only did they NOT do their jobs, but when the one inmate that FEARED for his life gave a passing officer his Inmate Request Form II-60| stating he needed to be moved because his cellmate was going to kill him. You can clearly see this lone piece of paper go through the hands of numerous Ranking Officers and others, before landing in the hands of a lone sergeant. Who read it and then did one of the stupidest things he could have ever done. Crumbled it up and threw it into the trash.

This lone sergeant was none other then SGT. Robert D. Schlageter. Let us not be pissed off at his actions alone, though they were bad, because he was the ONLY ONE TO TELL THE TRUTH. Lets look at a few things, shall we. One, why was SGT. Schlageter having to do a security check and count in the first place when his officers assigned to this Pod should have been doing them? Why, was he the last one to read over the Inmate Request Form (I-60) ,when other Rank higher them him had also read it and did nothing about it's warning? More importantly why is the state's most so-called secure prison in Texas so under staffed when it should have more then enough officers working, because it also houses Texas Death Row, which does NOT have enough staff to properly secure it and work it daily. And yet, those in Huntsville who oversee the Texas Department of Criminal Justice would have you believe everything is okay, when they too are full of shit.

Instead of bitching about what's going on in Texas Death Row (Deputy Director, Eric Guererro), and doing everything he can to make sure Death Row Prisoner's don't get certain apps on their Tablets such as the

Podcast for Mental Health, Movies, TV, Streaming Music, ect... your ass should be focusing on staff and staff that knows how to do a proper security check. Instead you have dicksuckers like John Whitmire and Brian Collier talking about how they see the end of Ad-Seg in the future, but instead are going out of your ways to fuck myself and others over, because you're so used to nobody pushing back against your injustice and abuse of power.

When SGT. Robert Schlageter came into work on Sunday, September 3rd, 2023 and told how he fucked up, when he was doing a security check on L-Pod. He failed to properly check on the inmates in #2 cage, even though the inmate in #1 cage told him, "Hey, there's a guy dead in that cage (meaning #2). He was thinking like everyone else that passed that cage, yeah, right. When he came to the door on #2 cage it was covered up, he asked verbally, how many? The answer was two, so he continued on with his count/security check. He admitted this to Investigator's and Director's. He told them, he fucked up, but why are we only firing one Ranking officer for telling the truth? What about investigating Warden Ronald S. Ivey and Major Vannessa Ward who oversees the General Population and lets it be known that this is their prison and they're here to take it back. And let us not forget the other fi e (5) officers besides SGT. Schlageter, why are they still working and not being punished for their lies and what the video footage shows???

So many questions, but not as many answers. It's NOT only the Texas Department of Criminal Justice that should be investigated, but the Office Inspector General too. I mean how is it even remotely possible that such a murder can take place at a so-called highly secured prison and not one time is it spoken about on the News anywhere? How do you cover up something so serious as if the death of this man, that could have been prevented, as if it doesn't matter. That his life wasn't important to his wife and family. He was set to go home to them in under thirty (30) fucking days, and you fuckers are doing everything within your abuse of power to cover it up and act like it didn't happen!

Explaining that the TDCJ-ID system wide lockdown is due in part because of the other sixteen homicide's throughout the State this year alone, when in truth that's BULLSHIT and your use to excuse this murder here and how YOU FUCKED UP! SGT.

Robert Schlageter is a Veteran and served his country in the United States

Military and when he speaks up and owns up to his fuck up, you walk him off the prison grounds, not caring about his three kids and wife and what he's done, when in truth you also should be held accountable for doing everything within your power to COVER UP this murder, letting other officers walk scot-free.

How come you're not sharing with society about the homicide that also took place in 7-Building on Labor Day weekend? You talk about cracking down and preventing contraband from coming into the prisons. You say its coming through the mail system so now we must get all our mail sent through a processing center, which will in turn forward it to our Tablets, and yet since you've started this Digital Mail, you have had MORE CONTRABAND AND DRUGS ENTERING INTO THE PRISON SYSTEM!

You've stopped visitation for Death Row prisoners saying we're part of the problem, but truth is, not only do we not get contact visits, but our visits are behind fucking glass and I haven't even seen my family because of fucking inhumane Restrictions for going on almost twenty fucking years! You had a prisoner escape from a chain us years ago and turn right around and punish Death Row by confiscating our Rhino Boots. Even though we are never supposed to be transported on a fucking bus but in a Van alone.

Whenever TD- CJ-ID fucks up it blames everyone else or comes up with some other fucking excuse. When 12- Building is under staffed which is where you house Texas Death Row prisoner's. instead of making sure this place has enough staff, you turn the fuck around and send our already short staffed officers to work out in the general population. Thus leaving officers on Death Row to have to work between two & three fucking Pods alone. You don't give them proper breaks and you fuck over the good ones just as much as you fuck us over, and now you wonder why so many fucking kinds of drugs are entering into the system. Don't act stupid because we already know how fucking stupid you truly are.

Let us not forget how you condone the actions of your officers being disrespectful towards all prisoner's, and when they step out there and are in the wrong, you not only let them, but turn right around and punish the prisoner for doing what so many others probably would have done or worse. What the fuck am I talking about? Friday, September 15th, 2023 on 4-Building Officer Downing (Female) was running off at the mouth being disrespectful to a prisoner in General Population, and though it could have been worse, all he did was give her a "Bitch slap" to wake her up and remind her where the fuck she's at. Now, instead of punishing her, you send the prisoner to 11-Building and are going to charge him with assault.

When will you start training your officer correctly in that they show respect to prisoners and their personal property when shaking us down during lockdowns?? You shake your heads, but let's back up and though again I don't agree with beating women, if they are going to put themselves into a situation where they know is bad and then do something to fuck over prisoner's and forget about it years or months down the road. When their actions could cast prisoner's more time added onto their sentences when they write bogus fucking cases.

Look at Offic r Whitsel back around 2013, she did some seriously fucked up shit and Karma caught up to her ass out in the General Population. She got her ass beat so fucking bad she was life flight d from here and had fucking boot prints on her chest and face from the two prisoners who beat her fucking ass.

You worry about contraband that you know your dirty officers are bringing inside the prisons, and yet you have prisoners over in 11-Building passing out from burning alive in there because the building has no air conditioning. Cells 1-9 are single celled and 10-51 are double celled and when the temps hit over 103° two weeks ago, it was 123° on 2-Row in 11-Building. Yet you can sit there and call us prisoners animals when in truth people like John Whitmire and Brian Collier, Deputy Director Eric Guerrero and others are the fucking Animals. You only tell society what you want them to hear, not what they should hear and see. That short timer that was so heartlessly murdered by his cellmate, the wife and family should sue the fuck out of TDCI-ID and Brian Collier, Deputy Director Eric Guerrero and John Whitmire.

I'm not going to make this book all about the dickheads like those above, but I always want to bring attention to the officers that do their jobs and are still working and being honest without going out of their ways to fuck prisoners and their families over. Not everyone is a fucking dickhead like you two John Whitmire and Deputy Director Eric Guererro!

RICHARD TABLER

CHAPTER 4
"Recognizing Real & Honest Officers"

Security Threat Group (STG), Officer J. Gomez. This is a man that stands out from most, because when I first met him he was just another correctional officer among all the rest. But over time, his actions along with his attitude to always treat everyone of us the same would stick. He never changed up, that's not to say that if you fucked up, he wouldn't help you straighten your fucking self up, because he would. But he never would go out of his way to write a bogus case or fuck someone over just because we were already in prison.

Having a sentence of Death isn't easy for those working here to face nor deal with us, if they're honest and sincere about themselves and their walk in life after they leave this place to return to their loved ones. I got to enjoy watching this Officer move up through the ranks and go from being a normal officer to doing something he wanted to do, which was become a part of STG (Security Threat Group. It's funny as I watch this guy walking and talking to other prisoners coming in on the chain buses left and right. He's got his ese swag down like some bad ass dude, who has a car in the parking lot, that he cannot wait to get back into and throw the switches! More people should see how an Officer should be by watching Officer Gomez.

This next person is very dear to me and I consider a friend, but because of my situation and hers, I'm only going to call her "Sheriff Deputy C.R.". This is to protect her from assholes reading this book and from her own boss possibly reading this book and looking at her differently because I write about her within these pages. This person has a heart of gold and though she worked at this prison for a short time, she left because she couldn't deal with all the asshole's and I'm NOT talking about the prisoner's but her own coworkers treating her and others like shit, because let me tell you She's not wrong, there are some women here wearing the uniform of a TDCJ Office , that give the new meaning to the word BITCH My love and respects to you and your boyfriend, "Sheriff Deputy C.R. "May you be richly blessed in all that you and your soon to be husband seek in your many years of life. I just want to drive your truck! Lol. I'm on the lookout for those that caused you bodily harm while doing your job outside these walls. Keep your head up and stay safe and take care of you know who.:)

Assistant Warden Darryl D, Sanders, this man is still fresh to this Unit (Prison) .One thing I have noticed unlike his co-worker Ronald S. Ivey. Is that Asst.Warden Darryl D.Sanders, does not enjoy it when you challenge his Word about something! He's doing a so/so job of keeping to his word. For now the Jury is still out on him, only time will tell how he does and if he's going to remain upstanding or become a fuck up, and a man that's word is no good.

Office , Shaith M. Amous, this muthafucker will work circles around your ass. He's dedicated and he's REAL. Serving a short stint in the Military back home. he's been working here at the Polunsky Unit for some time and was even awarded Officer of the Year by the Rank & File of this Unit. One thing I like about Officer Amous, is he's sincere about treating everyone the same. He doesn't go out of his way to fuck anyone over, and he doesn't drag his fucking ass when it's time to work. Plus, if you have a sincere problem, he will go out of his way and try to help you fix resolve the problem, by either taking care of it himself or speaking directly to the Rank. Like STG Officer Gomez. Officer Amous keeps it 100° all the time and treats everyone the same day in and day out without passing judgement upon anyone.

The below Officers can also be depended upon to do their Jobs when on the clock without complaining or taking it out on those of us wearing white here in Texas prisons:

Officer S. Bean, Officer V. Berry, Officer" TinkerBell Beck", SGT. J.Bey, Officer A. Cockrell, Major N. Neyland, Officer R.Davis (Kitchen) , Officer B.Alaniz, Mrs. Demarest, Officer J.Felipe, SGT.A.Goodrum, LT.A.Guidry, LT. B.Hindsman, Officer M. Marsh, Officer B. Peredes, Officer A. Moriarity, SGT.M. Portillo, LT.M. Ruble, Officer H.Sczech-Smith, Sara D.Sczech, Captain H.Watson, LT.T. Farris, SGT. J.Totin, Officer G. Yannazzo, Officer S.Vannazzo, Brandi Matthews, Captain

Hansen, Officer Owens, Officer A. Moore, Director D. Dickerson, Director Hazelwood, Director G.Hunter, Officer Rivas, Officer Nicoson, Officer M. C valcante.

My thanks to each of you for at one point in time or another crossing my path or having to deal with me and in doing so, being sincere and honest without going out of your way to fuck me over in some possible way because you wear a uniform and I am in white. More Officers should follow your examples and learn from you on how to behave and act within prison walls, because if they did so, they would learn and see how it feels to be RESPECTED, as each of you are by me and many others that refuse to speak up. Thank you, for treating me like a human being and not some fucking animal like those I've named in previous Chapters of this short book. May you all be safe and richly blessed through out your lives.

Richard Tabler

CHAPTER 5
"The End"

Before I close out this short book of mine. I'd like for each of you to think about something. You have two puppy's that you picked up from a shelter to bring home to your family or to your friends.

One of the puppies you give tender love to, and you play with him and feed him. You take him on walks or runs during the week, he plays with your family and becomes protective of those that have shown him such love and compassion. This is a puppy that will grow up to be a loving family dog or a dedicated dog to it's owner through out its life.

Now you take the other puppy, and you throw him into a cage. You don't feed him, and you leave him outside in all kinds of nasty weather. You beat his cage with a stick and sometimes, which is most of the times, you beat him too. This is a puppy that's going to grow into an aggressive dog. A dog that will only know how to do one thing, and that is bite and fuck off those who were always mistreating him. This isn't going to be a dog you're going to want to pet or play with ar take home to a loving family. This is a dog you're going to do everything you possibly can do to stay the fuck away from.

Think about how I and others are being treated within the Texas Department of Criminal Justice. When I show that I am capable of changing for the better, you allow someone to abuse their place of authority to fuck me and others over. Thus, though I could have very well ended up like the first puppy even while inside these prison walls and on Texas Death Row, I've sadly become the second puppy and right now I'd like nothing more then to fucking chew some fucking heads off.

The Texas Department of Criminal Justice just like the Judicial System through out the United States of America, only allows the following to take place within the Courts.... "Prosecutors are the devil incarnate. They don't try to hind out the circumstances that lead many of us to prison. Instead, they & in turn society define us by our worst mistakes we ever made in our lives, refusing to entertain any possible thought or motion that any of us can change. Until this way of thinking changes itself, those of us in prison like myself, will always be misunderstood by people like you.

Malik Al Mawt

Questions for the Author of this book, may be sent to:
Richard L. Tabler, #999523
Polunsky Unit/D.R.
Po. Box 660400
Dallas, TX. 75266-0400

" Malik-al-Mawt"
" Angel of Death "

You can also reach the Author for question's through the Securus Technologies Tablet, by opening up an account, so that we can mes-sage back and forth.

Previous titles: Within The Shadows of Life
                  Advice From A Dead Man

www.ingramcontent.com/pod-product-compliance
Ingram Content Group UK Ltd.
Pitfield, Milton Keynes, MK11 3LW, UK
UKHW061140180426

11947UKWH00004B/18